CELLO ▼ BOOK THREE

ESSENTIAL TECHNIQUE
FOR STRINGS

A COMPREHENSIVE STRING METHOD

MICHAEL ALLEN • ROBERT GILLESPIE • PAMELA TELLEJOHN HAYES

INTERMEDIATE TECHNIQUE STUDIES

THREE MAJOR SECTIONS

  I.   Higher Positions and Shifting
  II. Keys and Scales
  III. Bowings, Rhythms and Vibrato

Essential Technique for Strings is a book of studies to help the intermediate player develop the skills necessary for playing in an orchestra. Chronologically, it follows Book 2 of *Essential Elements for Strings;* however, it is designed as a multi-use technique book for use within a string orchestra setting. The various sections of the book are organized so that you may use them in the way that best suits your individual needs.

As you progress with your musical training you will become involved in a variety of performances. Always observe proper concert etiquette by being well prepared, dressing appropriately, being on time, and remembering all equipment. Show respect when others are playing by listening attentively and applauding at the appropriate time.

As your musical experiences continue, you will enjoy discussing various opportunities that are available to musicians. Careers include teaching, performing, conducting, and composing. No matter what profession you choose, there are always opportunities available to you to continue your musical involvement. You can continue to play your instrument in community, civic, or church orchestras. One can also attend concerts and become a supporter of the arts. Whether you choose music as a vocation or avocation, we hope it will always be an important part of your life. We wish you the very best for a lifetime of musical success.

To create an account, visit:
www.essentialelementsinteractive.com

Student Activation Code
"E3CE-4208-0361-8832"

ISBN 978-0-634-06931-4

HAL•LEONARD®
CORPORATION
7777 W. BLUEMOUND RD. P.O. BOX 13819 MILWAUKEE, WI 53213

THIRD, THIRD EXTENDED, AND FOURTH POSITIONS ON THE D STRING

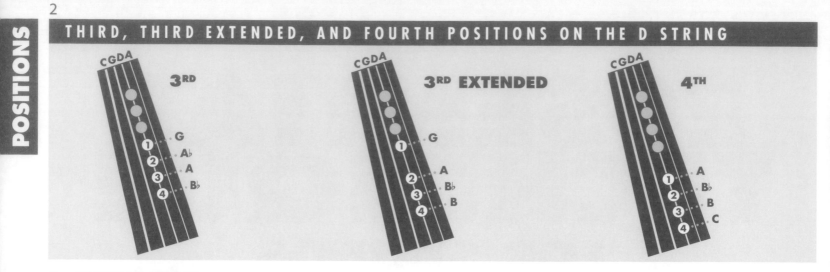

1. **TUNING TRACK**

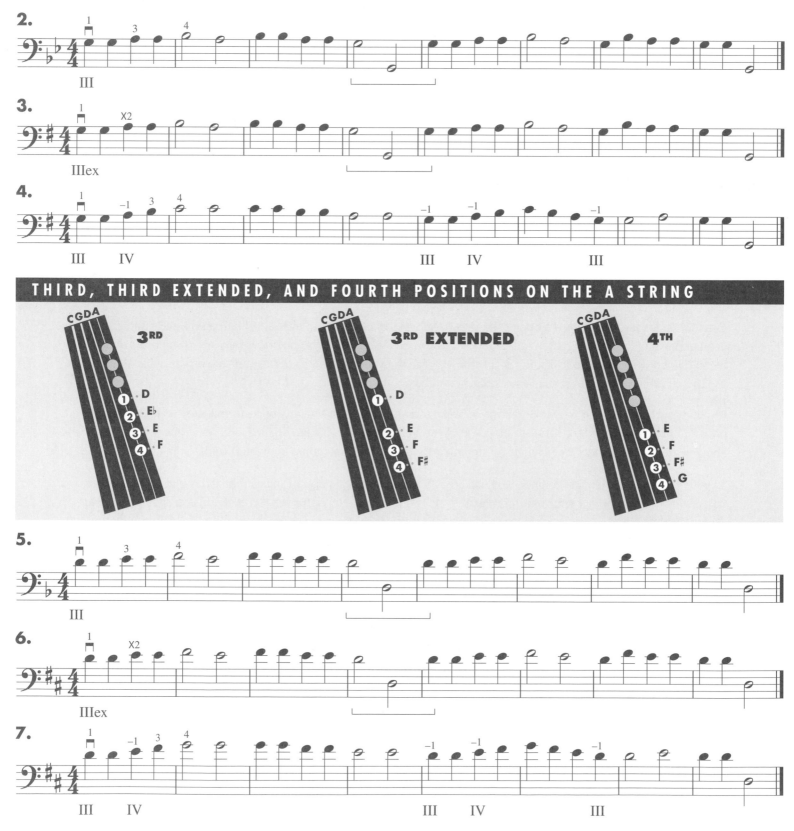

THIRD, THIRD EXTENDED, AND FOURTH POSITIONS ON THE A STRING

8.

9. *Write the correct finger numbers for fourth (IV) position below each note.*

10.

11. FRENCH FOLK SONG

Moderato

The **symphony** has its roots in late 18th century central Europe. Haydn, a German composer, wrote more than one hundred symphonies and is credited with setting a standard of symphonic composition that was a model for those who followed. Haydn's contemporary, Mozart, added to the symphony by expanding melodic content as well as form. Beethoven brought the symphony into the Romantic age by further expanding form as well as changing instrumentation. Following Beethoven were numerous Romantic composers such as Tchaikovsky, Brahms, and Dvořák who developed harmony, rhythm, and folk elements.

By the late 1800s, Mahler's and Bruckner's compositions were so developed that they hardly resembled the symphonies of Haydn. Listen to recordings of symphonies from various style periods and attend live performances whenever possible. Describe the various sounds and instruments that you hear.

12. SYMPHONY NO. 1 THEME

Allegro   Gustav Mahler (1860–1911)

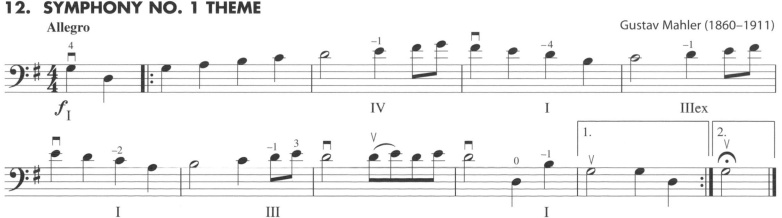

Natural Harmonic
(Review)

Natural harmonics are tones created by a vibrating string divided into equal sections. To play an octave higher than an open string, lightly touch the string exactly half way between the bridge and the nut. In the following examples, harmonics are indicated by a "○" above a note, plus a fingering number. $\overset{3}{\circ}$ indicates a harmonic played with the third finger.

13.

14.

15.
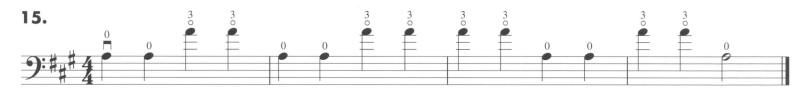

16.
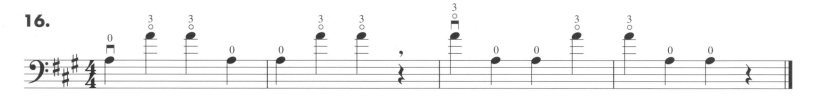

Shifting
(Review)

Slide your left hand smoothly and lightly to a new location on the fingerboard, indicated by a dash (–). Be sure your thumb moves with your hand.

17.

18.

19.

20.

SHIFTING ON THE D AND A STRINGS

21.

22.

23.

24.

25.

26.

27.

28.

FOURTH AND FOURTH EXTENDED POSITIONS ON THE D STRING

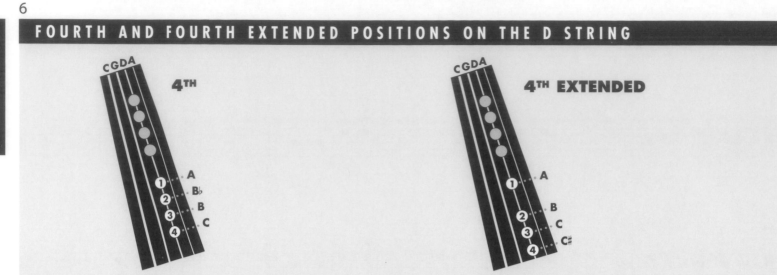

29.

IV

30.

IVex

31.

IVex   IVex   IVex

32.

IVex   IVex   I

33.

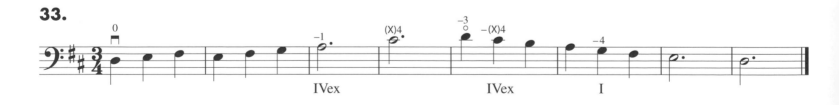

IVex   IVex   I

34.

IVex   I   IVex

35. CAN CAN

Presto ◁ *Very fast*   Jacques Offenbach (1819–1880)

D.S. al Fine — Play until you see the **D.S. al Fine**. Then go back to the sign (𝄋) and play until the word **Fine**. D.S. is the abbreviation for **Dal Segno**, or "from the sign," and **Fine** means "the end."

36. MARCH IN D

Marziale ◁ *March-like style*   Johann Sebastian Bach (1685–1750)

SHIFTING ON THE D STRING

37.

38.

39.

40.

SHIFTING ON THE D STRING

41.

42.

43.

44.

45.

46.

47.

48.

SHIFTING ON THE A STRING

49.

50.

51.

52.

53.

54.

55.

56.

THIRD, THIRD EXTENDED, AND FOURTH POSITIONS ON THE G STRING

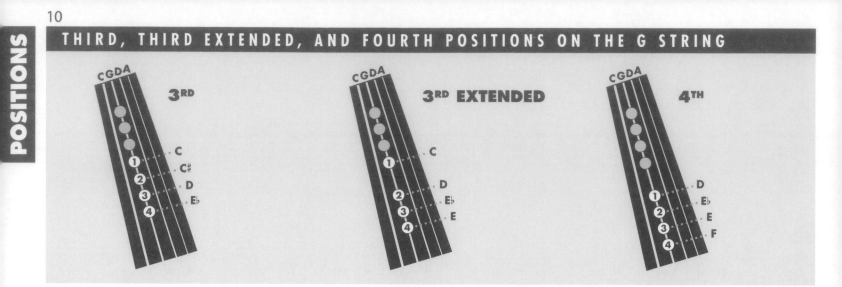

57.

58.

59.

60.

61.

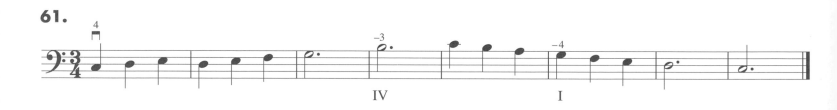

62.

Rallentando   *rall.* – Gradually slower (same as *ritardando*).

63. LONG LONG AGO

64. BLUE BELLS OF SCOTLAND

SHIFTING ON THE G STRING

65.

66.

67.

68.

SECOND, SECOND EXTENDED, AND SECOND 1/2 POSITIONS ON THE D AND A STRINGS

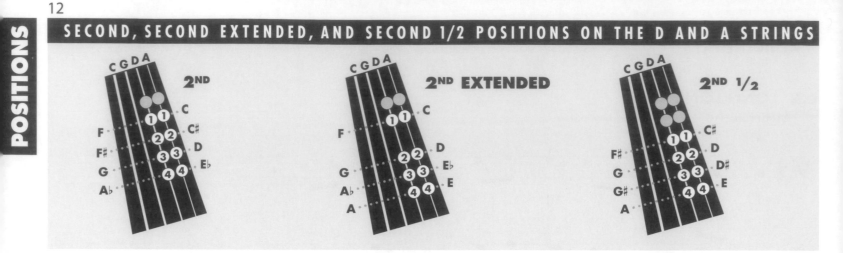

69.

70.

71.

72.

73.

74.

75.

76.

77.

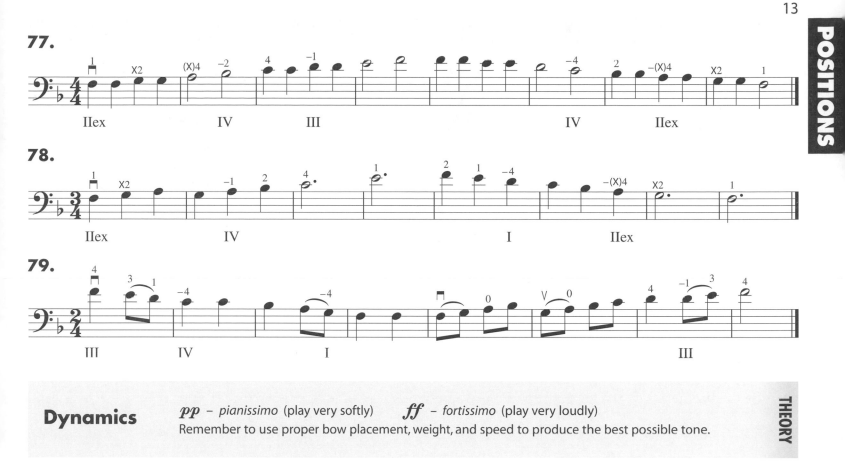

78.

79.

Dynamics   *pp* – *pianissimo* (play very softly)   *ff* – *fortissimo* (play very loudly)
Remember to use proper bow placement, weight, and speed to produce the best possible tone.

80. ROW, ROW, ROW YOUR BOAT – Round

Moderato   Traditional

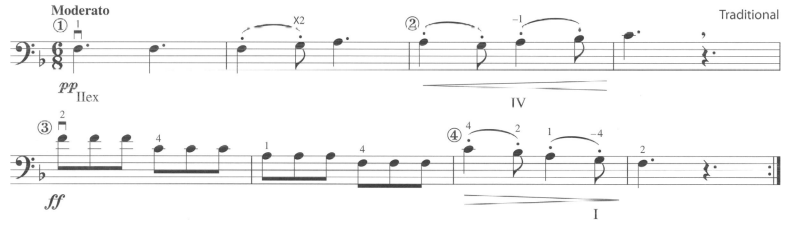

A **Concerto** is a composition in several movements for solo instrument and orchestra. Exercise 81 is the theme from the first movement of the *Concerto for Violin and Orchestra* by **Ludwig van Beethoven**, composed while author William Wordsworth was writing his poem *I Wandered Lonely as a Cloud*. A special feature of the concerto is the cadenza, which was improvised, or made up, by the soloist during a concert. Improvising and creating your own music is great fun. Try it if you have not already.

81. THEME FROM VIOLIN CONCERTO

Andante   Ludwig van Beethoven (1770–1827)

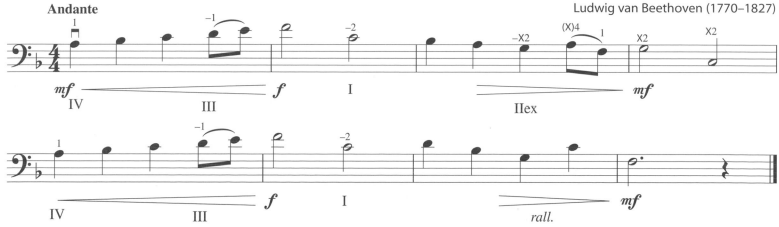

THIRD, THIRD EXTENDED, AND FOURTH POSITIONS ON THE C STRING

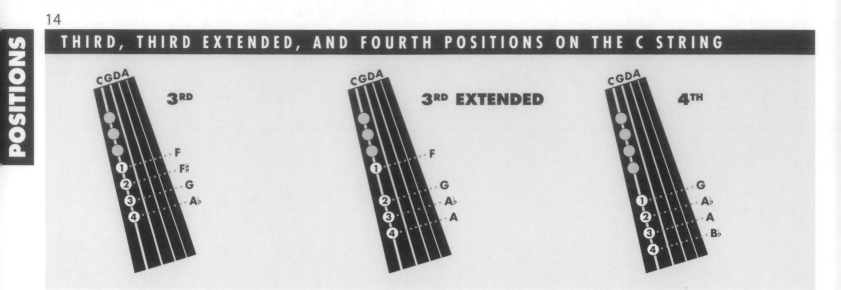

82.

83.

84.

85.

86.

87.

88. OH! SUSANNAH

Allegretto

Stephen C. Foster (1826–1864)

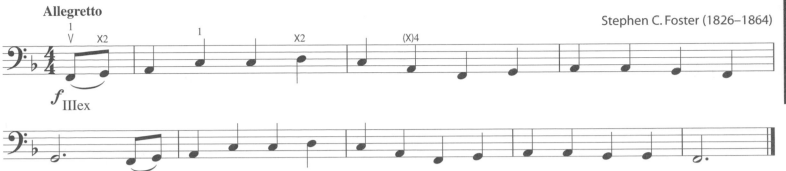

Music can be created and arranged by changing rhythms and notes of an existing example. Create your own arrangement of *Oh! Susannah* by changing the rhythms and melodic phrases. Perform your arrangement for others.

Example 1: Changing rhythms   *Example 2: Changing melodic phrases*

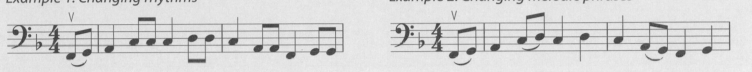

89. FIELD SONG

Moderato

Southern American Folk Song

SHIFTING ON THE C STRING

90.

91.

92.

93.

POSITIONS

THIRD, THIRD EXTENDED, AND FOURTH POSITIONS ON THE D STRING (review)

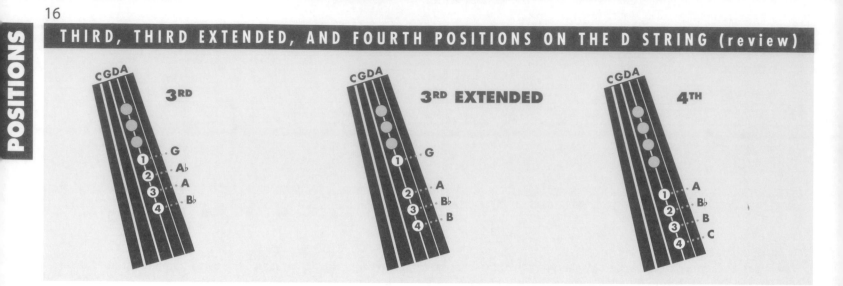

94.

95.

96.

97.

98.

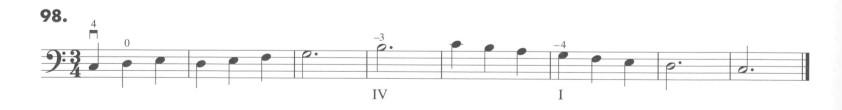

99.

100. JOLLY GOOD FELLOW

Moderato

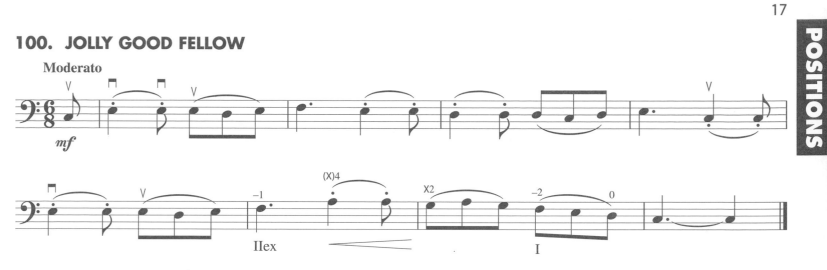

Copy exercise 100 on a piece of manuscript paper. Be sure to include the time signature, dynamics, and bowings.

101. MAY TIME

W. A. Mozart (1756–1791)

Allegretto

SHIFTING ON THE A AND D STRINGS

102.

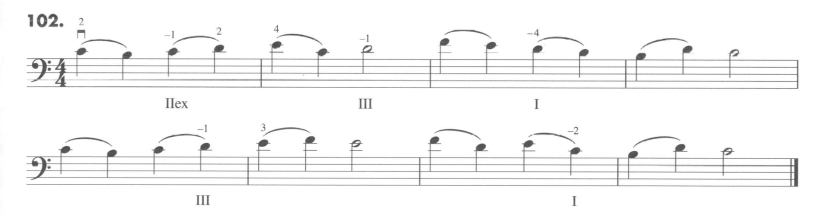

103.

C MAJOR

104. FINGER PATTERNS IN C MAJOR *(violin, viola)*

105. FINGER PATTERNS IN C MAJOR *(violin, viola)*

Identify two important elements of performing scales and arpeggios accurately. As you play each of these in the various keys presented in this section, check to make sure you are able to do these things.

106. C MAJOR SCALE

107. C MAJOR ARPEGGIO

108. THIRDS IN C MAJOR

109. THE BRITISH GRENADIERS

English

Allegro

Johann Sebastian Bach is probably best remembered as an organist and church musician, but he also wrote hundreds of compositions for the royal courts of Germany and Austria. For example, *The Brandenburg Concertos* are works for instrumental ensembles dedicated to the court at Brandenburg. Bach lived at the same time the original thirteen colonies were being settled by European immigrants. The chorales in this book can be performed by the entire orchestra, or a small ensemble. Following any performance, always evaluate your playing and make a list of things to improve.

110. CHORALE IN C

A = Melody. **B** = Harmony.

J. S. Bach (1685–1750)

G MAJOR

111. FINGER PATTERNS IN G MAJOR *(violin, viola)*

112. FINGER PATTERNS IN G MAJOR *(violin, viola)*

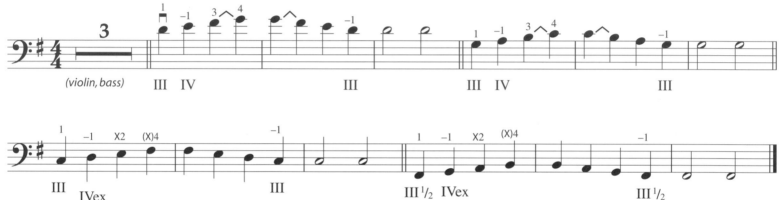

113. G MAJOR SCALE

114. G MAJOR ARPEGGIO *Identify the intervals before playing.*

115. THIRDS IN G MAJOR

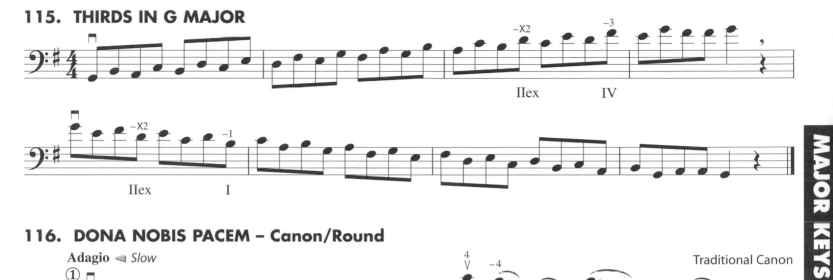

IIex   IV

IIex   I

116. DONA NOBIS PACEM – Canon/Round

Traditional Canon

II ½   I

III   I

117. CHORALE IN G   A = Melody. B = Harmony.

J. S. Bach (1685–1750)

MAJOR KEYS

D MAJOR

118. FINGER PATTERNS IN D MAJOR *(violin, viola)*

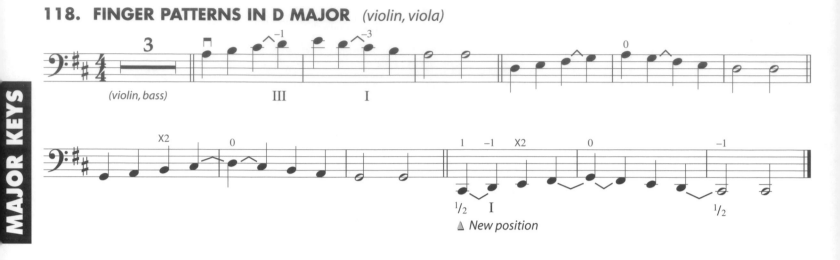

119. FINGER PATTERNS IN D MAJOR *(violin, viola)*

120. D MAJOR SCALE

121. D MAJOR ARPEGGIO

122. THIRDS IN D MAJOR

123. TRUMPET VOLUNTARY

Jeremiah Clarke (1674–1707)

Maestoso ◁ *Bold, stately*

124. CHORALE IN D

A = Melody. **B** = Harmony.

J. S. Bach (1685–1750)

A MAJOR

125. FINGER PATTERNS IN A MAJOR *(violin, viola)*

126. FINGER PATTERNS IN A MAJOR *(violin, viola)*

127. A MAJOR SCALE *Mark all the half steps before playing.*

128. A MAJOR ARPEGGIO

129. THIRDS IN A MAJOR

130. THE YELLOW ROSE OF TEXAS

131. CHORALE IN A   A = Melody. B = Harmony.

J. S. Bach (1685–1750)

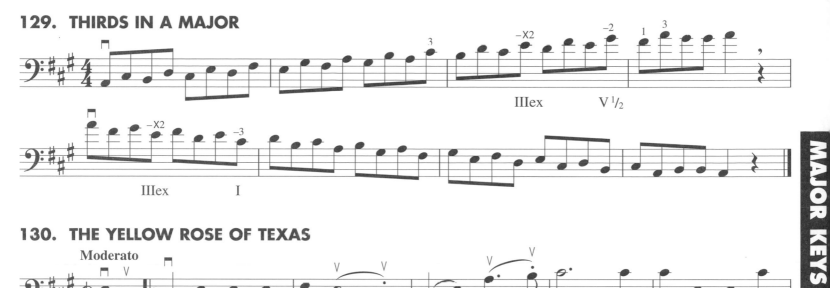

F MAJOR

132. FINGER PATTERNS IN F MAJOR *(violin, viola)*

(violin, bass)

133. FINGER PATTERNS IN F MAJOR *(violin, viola)*

(violin, bass)

134. F MAJOR SCALE

135. F MAJOR ARPEGGIO

136. THIRDS IN F MAJOR

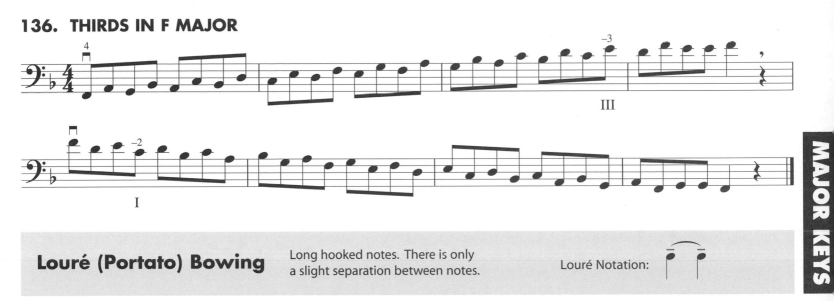

III

I

Louré (Portato) Bowing   Long hooked notes. There is only a slight separation between notes.   Louré Notation:

---

137. SIMPLE GIFTS

Shaker Melody

Moderato

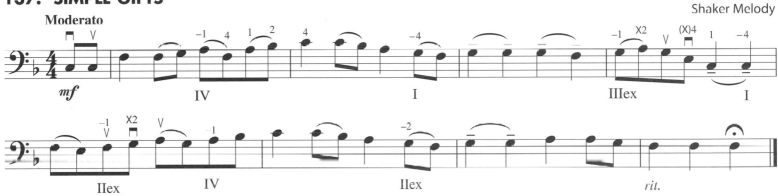

mf   IV   I   IIIex   I

IIex   IV   IIex   *rit.*

---

138. CHORALE IN F   **A** = Melody. **B** = Harmony.

J. S. Bach (1685–1750)

A   *mf* IIex   IV   IIex

B   *mf*

A   III   IIex   III   IIex

B

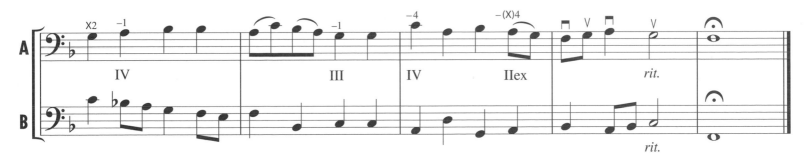

A   IV   III   IV   IIex   *rit.*

B   *rit.*

MAJOR KEYS

B♭ MAJOR

139. FINGER PATTERNS IN B♭ MAJOR *(violin, viola)*

(violin, bass)

140. FINGER PATTERNS IN B♭ MAJOR *(violin, viola)*

(violin, bass)

141. B♭ MAJOR SCALE

New position

142. B♭ MAJOR ARPEGGIO

New position

MAJOR KEYS

143. THIRDS IN B♭ MAJOR

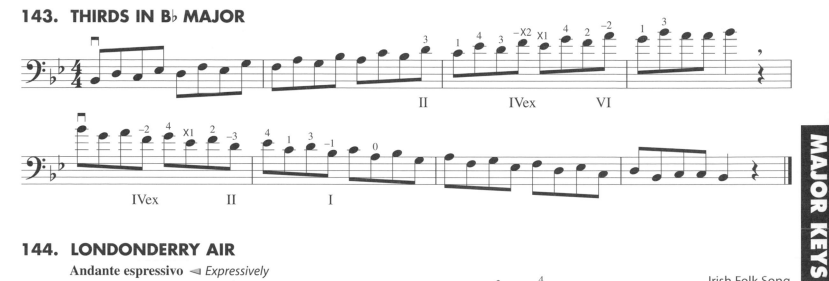

144. LONDONDERRY AIR

Andante espressivo ◁ *Expressively*

Irish Folk Song

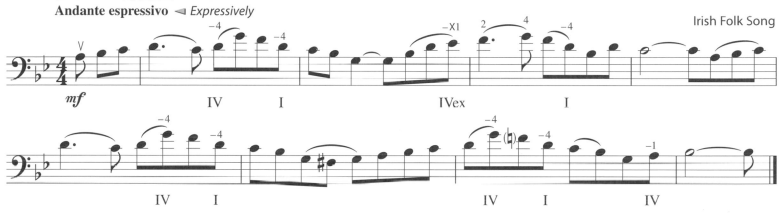

145. CHORALE IN B♭

A = Melody. **B** = Harmony.

J. S. Bach (1685–1750)

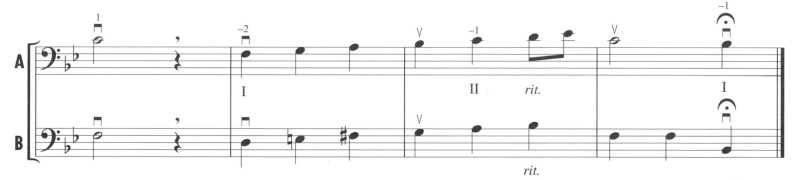

E♭ MAJOR

146. FINGER PATTERNS IN E♭ MAJOR *(violin, viola)*

147. FINGER PATTERNS IN E♭ MAJOR *(violin, viola)*

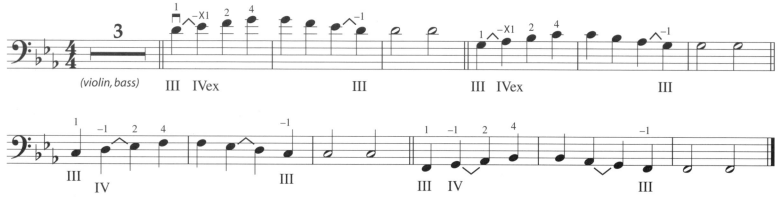

148. E♭ MAJOR SCALE

149. E♭ MAJOR ARPEGGIO

150. THIRDS IN E♭ MAJOR

German composer **Richard Wagner** was one of the leading opera writers in the mid to late 1800s. He brought musical drama to a new height with elaborate sets, large orchestras, and longer lengths of performance. His goal was to create a new art form where music and drama were of equal importance. During the same time, the first railroads were being built, the Americans fought a civil war, and Alexander Graham Bell invented the telephone.

151. PILGRIM'S CHORUS FROM TANNHÄUSER

Richard Wagner (1813–1883)

152. CHORALE IN E♭

A = Melody. **B** = Harmony.

J. S. Bach (1685–1750)

A MINOR

Minor Keys

Minor keys and their scales sound different from major keys because of their different pattern of whole and half steps. Each minor key is *relative* or "related" to the major key with the same key signature.

The simplest form of a minor key is called **natural minor**. Two other types are **harmonic minor** and **melodic minor**, each of which have certain altered tones.

153. A NATURAL MINOR

154. A HARMONIC MINOR

▲ New position

155. A MELODIC MINOR

156. A MINOR ARPEGGIO

157. SCARBOROUGH FAIR

Andante

158. GREENSLEEVES *Identify which form of the minor scale is used in this exercise.*

Andante

English Folk Tune

E MINOR

159. E NATURAL MINOR

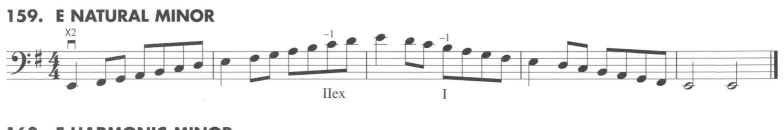

160. E HARMONIC MINOR

161. E MELODIC MINOR

162. E MINOR ARPEGGIO

163. LA CINQUANTAINE

Gabriel Marie (1852–1882)

164. BOURÉE FROM SUITE IN E MINOR FOR LUTE

J.S. Bach (1685–1750)

MINOR KEYS

D MINOR

165. D NATURAL MINOR

166. D HARMONIC MINOR

167. D MELODIC MINOR

168. D MINOR ARPEGGIO

169. HEY, HO! NOBODY HOME – Round

Memorize this round. Then perform it for the class with a friend.

Traditional English

Musical Form — Musical form refers to how a piece of music is organized. One common form, ABA, is used in exercise 170. The first and third lines are the same (A) while the second line is different (B).

170. ZUM GALI GALI

Israeli Folk Tune

G MINOR

171. G NATURAL MINOR

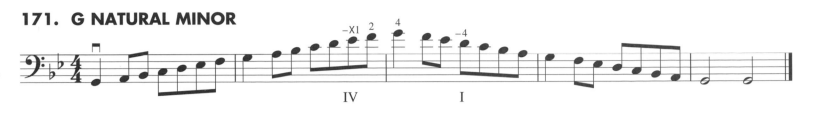

172. G HARMONIC MINOR

173. G MELODIC MINOR

174. G MINOR ARPEGGIO

Spirituals are religious folk songs originating within the African-American community. They were originally associated with work, recreation, or religious gatherings. Spirituals remain popular today, probably due to their strong rhythmic character and melodic lines.

175. JOSHUA

African-American Spiritual

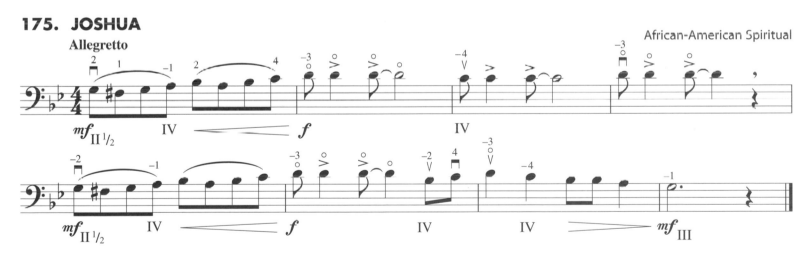

176. PAT-A-PAN

French Carol

C MINOR

177. C NATURAL MINOR

178. C HARMONIC MINOR

179. C MELODIC MINOR

180. C MINOR ARPEGGIO

HISTORY

Czech composer **Bedrich Smetana** was one of several 19th century composers who infused native folk themes into his compositions. "Moldau," named for a river in Bohemia, is one theme that is part of a collection of songs, entitled *Má Vlast* or " My Homeland." While composers of the 19th century were returning to their folk roots for inspiration, artists and writers were turning to more realistic reflections of current society. Charles Dickens was writing *David Copperfield* and *A Tale of Two Cities,* and Vincent van Gogh and Claude Monet both created images of urban and country life.

181. MOLDAU

Bedrich Smetana (1824–1884)

HISTORY

A gavotte is a refined dance style in $\frac{2}{2}$ or $\frac{2}{4}$ from the Baroque Era (1600–1750).

182. GAVOTTE

J.S. Bach (1685–1750)

Enharmonics

Enharmonics are two different note names which are both the same pitch *(see page 47 for more examples).*

G# = A♭

183. ABA DABA

Allegretto

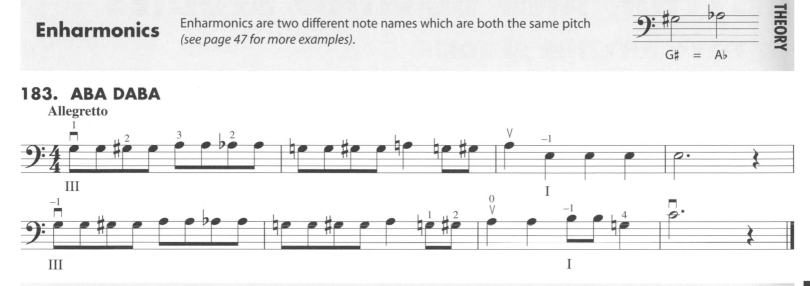

A **Habañera** is a Cuban dance and song form in slow 2/4 meter. It is named after the city of Havana, the capital of Cuba. Made popular in the New World in the early 19th century, it was later carried over to Spain. In Spain, the rhythms of the Habañera were incorporated into many styles of Latin music. One of the most famous Habañeras is heard in Bizet's *Carmen,* written in 1875.

184. HABAÑERA

Georges Bizet (1838–1875)

Moderato

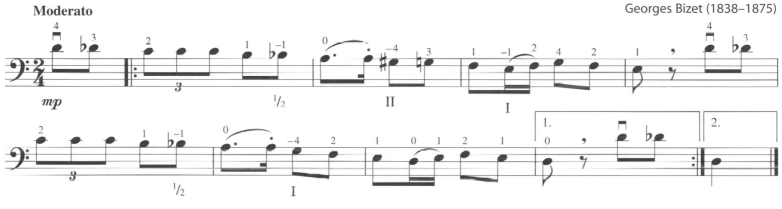

Chromatic Scale

A chromatic scale is made up of consecutive half steps. It is usually written with sharps (♯) going up and flats (♭) going down.

185. SHIFTING CHROMATIC FINGERING

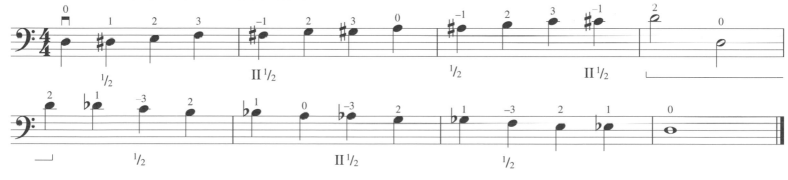

186. CHROMATIC ETUDE

RHYTHM AND BOWING STUDIES

DOTTED RHYTHM STUDIES

NOTE DURATION CHART

1 e & a 2 e & a 3 e & a 4 e & a

187. *Write the counts below the notes before playing.*

188.

189.

190.

191.

192.

Sight-reading

Sight-reading means playing a musical piece for the first time. Review the word **S-T-A-R-S** to remind yourself what to look for before you play.

S — **Sharps or flats** in the key signature
T — **Time signature** and **tempo markings**
A — **Accidentals** not found in the key signature
R — **Rhythms**, silently counting the more difficult notes and rests
S — **Signs**, including dynamics, articulations, repeats and endings

Now sight-read the following exercise.

193.

RHYTHMS & BOWINGS

SIXTEENTH NOTE STUDIES

NOTE DURATION CHART

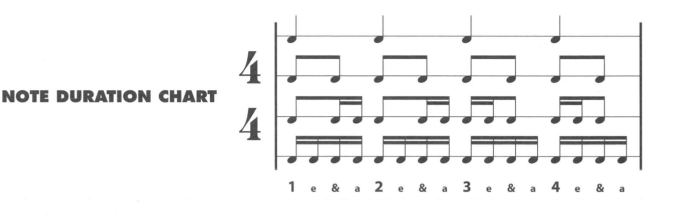

1 e & a 2 e & a 3 e & a 4 e & a

194. *Write the counts below the notes before playing.*

195.

196.

197.

198.

199.

Review **S-T-A-R-S** before sight-reading the following exercise.

200.

SYNCOPATION STUDIES

NOTE DURATION CHART

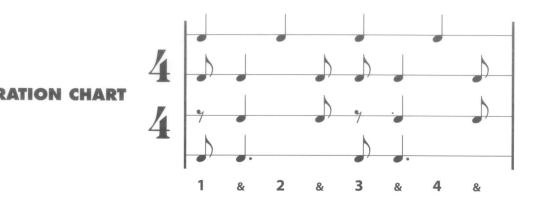

201. *Write the counts below the notes before playing.*

202.

203.

204.

205.

206.

Review **S-T-A-R-S** before sight-reading the following exercise.

207.

6/8 RHYTHM STUDIES

NOTE DURATION CHART

208. *Write the counts below the notes before playing.*

209.

210.

211.

212.

213.

Review **S-T-A-R-S** before sight-reading the following exercise.

214.

RHYTHMS & BOWINGS

VIBRATO WORKOUTS

You can add beauty and feeling to your sound with VIBRATO, a smooth pulsation of the tone. It is created by varying the pitch slightly. Try these vibrato Workouts as directed by your teacher. Once you have mastered this skill, add vibrato to your solo and ensemble playing.

1. The Slide
Place your second finger on the A string. Slide up and down the string, covering the distance of 3 half-steps, then 2 half-steps, and finally 1 half-step. Your thumb should slide with the hand. Try this motion while using long, sustained bow strokes.

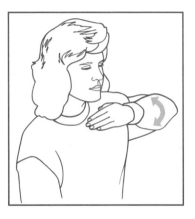

2. The Pivot
Touch the second finger of your left hand to your collarbone. Then pivot (rotate) your arm while keeping the elbow relatively still.

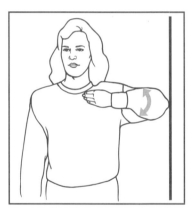

To check the motion away from the instrument, touch your elbow to the wall while doing The Pivot.

3. Pivot And Bow
Continue doing The Pivot motion, while playing long tones on open strings.

4. Vibrato
With your left thumb behind the neck, place your second finger on C on the A string and vibrate while playing a long, sustained bow stroke. Continue with third finger on C♯, then first finger on B, and finally with fourth finger on D.

VIBRATO

 Master these Workouts before using VIBRATO in your playing!

VIBRATO EXERCISES

First practice these vibrato exercises without bowing. The lower part of the vibrato motion is shown in small notes, which do not denote actual pitches. You may proceed with the bow once your teacher has approved your left hand motion.

215.

216.

217.

218.

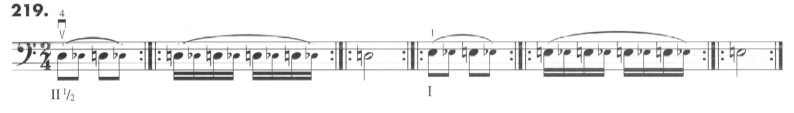

219.

220.

221.

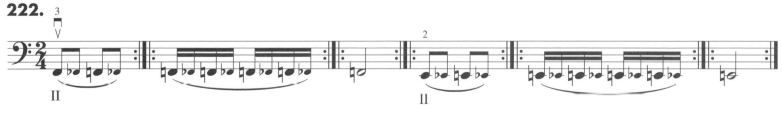

222.

223.

Spiccato Bowing

A light bouncing stroke in the lower half of the bow. Play spiccato (off the string) or staccato (on the string) as directed by your teacher. Spiccato is normally used in medium and faster tempos.

Spiccato Notation:

224.

225.

226.

227.

228. SLAVIC FOLK SONG

Allegretto

229.

230. CAN CAN

Jacques Offenbach (1819–1880)

Presto

FOR CELLOS ONLY

TENOR CLEF PRACTICE

A.

Name each note: D ___ ___ ___ ___ ___ ___ ___ ___

BASIC THUMB POSITION – D STRING   ## BASIC THUMB POSITION – A STRING

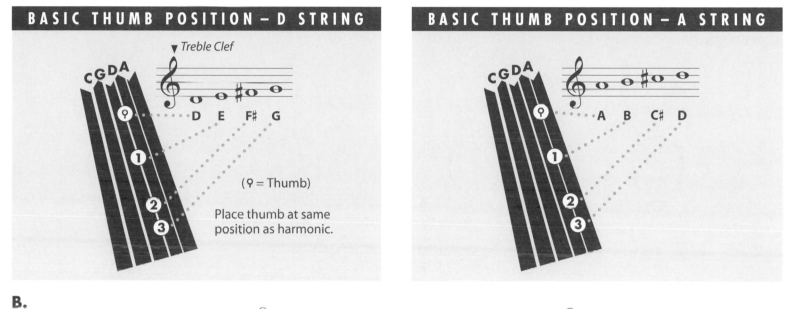

B.

HALF POSITION

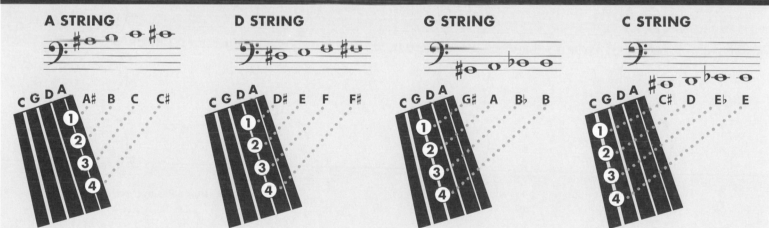

C.

D.

CELLO FINGERING CHART

Positions: ½ – I – II – III – IV

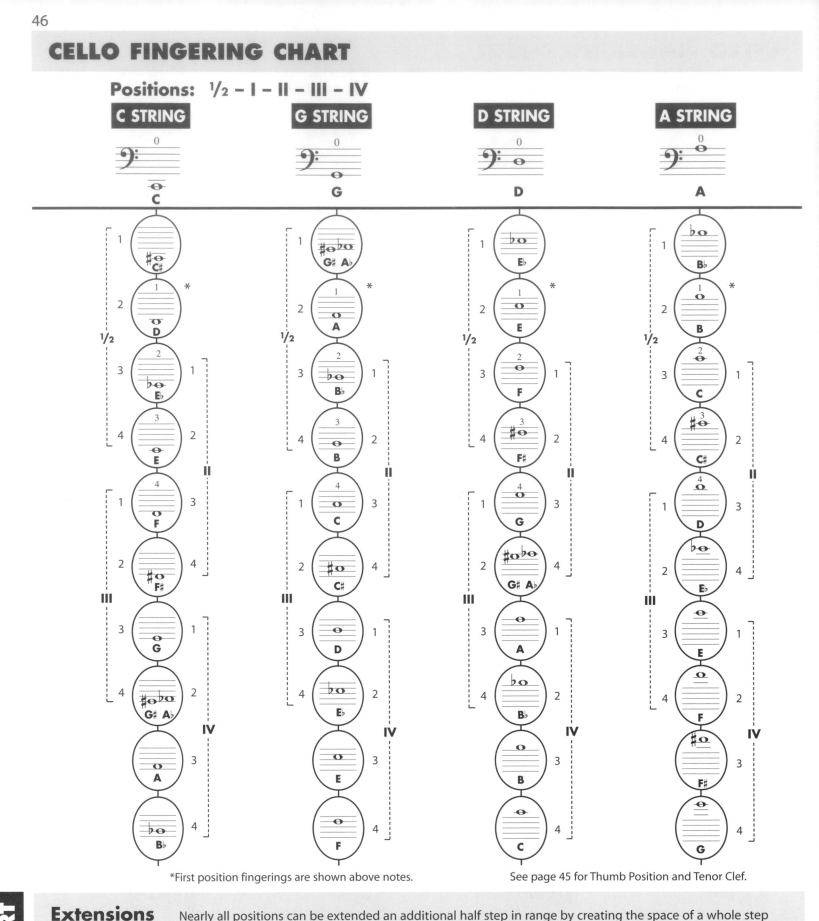

*First position fingerings are shown above notes.

See page 45 for Thumb Position and Tenor Clef.

Extensions

Nearly all positions can be extended an additional half step in range by creating the space of a whole step between the 1st and 2nd fingers. Although they look similar, there are important differences between Forward Extensions and Backward Extensions:

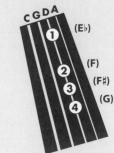

Forward Extension

• 1st finger remains in normal position.

• Other fingers each play a half step higher note than normal.

Backward Extension

• 1st finger plays a half step lower than normal.

• Other fingers remain in normal position.

FINGERING CHART

CELLO FINGERING CHART

Positions: I – II½ – III½ – Harmonics

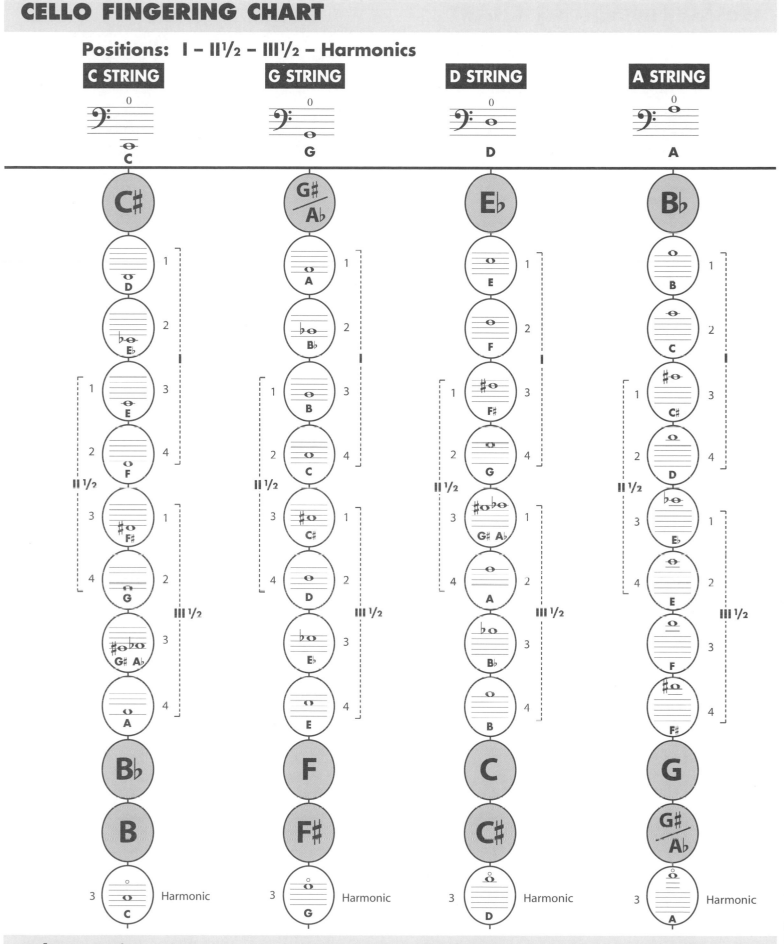

Enharmonics All sharps and flats have enharmonics which are usually played at the same place on the string, but may be played by a different finger. For example, a G♯ on the D string is played by 3rd finger in 2nd ½ position. The G♯ is at the same spot where A♭ is played by 2nd finger in 3rd position. Common enharmonics:

C♯ D♭   D♯ E♭   E F♭   E♯ F   F♯ G♭   G♯ A♭   A♯ B♭   B C♭   B♯ C

Composition

Composition is the art of writing original music. A composer often begins by creating a melody made up of individual **phrases**, like short musical "sentences." Some melodies have phrases that seem to answer or respond to "question" phrases.

Q. AND A. *Write your own "answer" to the following melodies.*

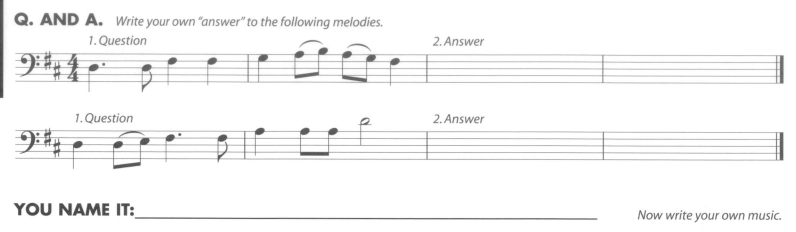

YOU NAME IT: _____

Now write your own music.

REFERENCE INDEX